Charles & Camilla

Foreword

A ROYAL WEDDING is a milestone in the life of the nation at any time. When the bridegroom is heir to the throne, it takes on an added significance, because the bride becomes the second most important woman in the country. Prince Charles' wife, the Duchess of Cornwall, has precedence over all other women in Britain apart from Her Majesty the Queen.

Although Camilla has been in the public eye for many years, it was previously as a private person. On 9 April 2005, she assumed the mantle of Royal responsibility that accompanies anyone who marries into the Royal Family. Already well used to the publicity that being a companion to the Prince of Wales meant, her life is now lived in the goldfish bowl that other members of the Royal Family have known throughout their lives. It is a prospect not every woman would welcome, but the Duchess knows that Prince Charles needs a strong, supporting partner and she is determined to help him with his public duties, while providing a happy personal life at home. They complement each other perfectly, work as a team and look forward to many contented years together.

Their relationship has matured into a comfortable partnership with each being aware of the other's contribution to its success.

The Duchess of Cornwall enjoys the respect of the Prince of Wales' household. Her sunny disposition, combined with a down-to-earth manner, benefits those who work with the Prince. He recognizes the value of his Duchess; her loyalty is unquestioned and her genuine interest in people apparent to all who meet her. The couple share a concern for the environment, the arts and the plight of the less fortunate. Their London home, Clarence House, has become the centre of the capital's Society, with Camilla the consummate hostess.

Together Prince Charles and Camilla are a formidable team, determined to overcome the challenges that may face them in the 21st century.

A Royal wedding

IN BEST ROMANTIC TRADITION, His Royal Highness Prince Charles proposed marriage to Camilla Parker Bowles, offering as his pledge of affection a Royal Family heirloom, a sparkling platinum and diamond ring.

The proposal followed the Prince's formal request to his mother, Her Majesty the Queen. The Queen and the Duke of Edinburgh offered their congratulations with their approval of the marriage.

Among the first messages of goodwill came those from Princes William and Harry, offering their hopes of happiness for their father and Mrs Parker Bowles.

At a reception and dinner held at Windsor Castle on the evening of their engagement, the couple's feelings for each other were evident and Camilla showed the guests – and the media – her engagement ring.

The spring wedding went ahead as planned – although the ceremonies at Windsor were postponed for one day while Prince Charles attended the funeral of Pope John Paul II in Rome. But the day's delay brought fine weather and a crowd of well-wishers as the Prince and Camilla were married in a civil ceremony at the imposing 300-year-old Guildhall at Windsor, a building completed by Sir Christopher Wren, whose father was the Dean of Windsor. A service of prayer and dedication in St George's Chapel, Windsor Castle, attended by family and friends, was led by Dr Rowan Williams, the Archbishop of Canterbury, who blessed Prince Charles and his new bride. A reception for the Royal couple and their guests followed in Windsor Castle's state apartments.

Prince Charles has many titles, some of which are automatically shared with his wife. As well as Prince of Wales and Duke of Cornwall he is Duke of Rothesay, Earl of Carrick, Baron Renfrew, Lord of the Isles and Great Prince of Scotland. Camilla is now known as the Duchess of Cornwall, using the title Duchess of Rothesay in Scotland. She is also granted the title Her Royal Highness and will be known as Princess Consort when her husband becomes King.

St George's Chapel at Windsor Castle has a special place in the hearts of the Royal Family. Its full name is The Queen's Free Chapel of St George – the word 'free' meaning that it does not come under the jurisdiction of any bishop, but of the Sovereign. Kings and queens of England have worshipped here for more than 500 years and for many, including the late Queen Mother, it is their final resting place.
Prince Charles' younger brother Prince Edward married Sophie Rhys-Jones at St George's Chapel in 1999 while, seven years earlier, Lady Helen Windsor chose the chapel as her wedding venue.

St George's Chapel, at the heart of important Royal occasions for more than 500 years, comes directly under the jurisdiction of Her Majesty the Queen.

The Prince of Wales and the Duchess of Cornwall leave St George's Chapel after the service of prayer and dedication on their wedding day, 9 April 2005.

The Prince of Wales and his bride-to-be appear relaxed and happy as they announce their engagement at Windsor Castle.

The quire and chancel of St George's Chapel where the newly married couple received a blessing from the Archbishop of Canterbury.

The Royal couple exchanged wedding rings made out of Welsh gold, following a tradition established by the Queen Mother in 1923.

Prince Charles' formal request to The Queen before proposing marriage to Camilla was a requirement of the Royal Marriages Act of 1772 which states that any lineal descendant of George II must obtain the consent of the Sovereign in order to marry.

Prince Charles gave his bride-to-be a classic 1920s platinum and diamond ring which once belonged to his grandmother, the late Queen Elizabeth the Queen Mother. A large square-cut diamond is flanked on each side by three smaller rectangular diamonds, or baguettes, down each shoulder. The shank and the setting are platinum. When it was made the ring would have been at the cutting edge of fashion and it is of a style that, more than 80 years later, is once more popular and desirable.

Prince Charles, heir to the throne

CHARLES PHILIP ARTHUR GEORGE, eldest son of Her Majesty the Queen and Prince Philip, Duke of Edinburgh, was born at Buckingham Palace late in the evening of 14 November 1948. His mother, Her Royal Highness Princess Elizabeth at the time of his birth, was proclaimed Queen Elizabeth II when her father, King George VI, died on 6 February 1952. Prince Charles, just three years old, became heir apparent to the throne.

He was now Duke of Cornwall and took the Scottish title Duke of Rothesay. When he was nine years old and a boarder at Cheam School, near Newbury in Berkshire, The Queen created him Prince of Wales and Earl of Chester.

It wasn't until he was 20 and a student at Cambridge University, where he studied archaeology and anthropology at Trinity, that his formal Investiture as Prince of Wales took place at Caernarfon Castle. Charles, entering fully into his role, spent some time beforehand at the University College of Wales at Aberystwyth, learning the Welsh language. In a colourful and moving ceremony his mother invested him as Prince of Wales on 1 July 1969.

The following year, when he was 21, Prince Charles took his seat in the House of Lords.

The Queen and the Duke of Edinburgh had broken with tradition by sending their eldest son to Gordonstoun, the school near Elgin in eastern Scotland, rather than having a tutor at Buckingham Palace. They both felt that he should mix with children from non-royal backgrounds. But, despite this relative informality, the Prince developed a strong sense of duty. He has always known that the country he will one day rule as King must come first, and he embarked on a career in the Armed Services after completing his studies.

Already a keen amateur pilot with a private licence, the Prince flew himself to Cranwell in Lincolnshire in March 1971 to start his four-month attachment with the Royal Air Force. Flight Lieutenant The Prince of Wales was awarded his RAF wings at Cranwell in August 1971.

The following month Charles joined the Royal Naval College, Dartmouth, as Acting Sub-Lieutenant. His father and great-uncle Earl Mountbatten of Burma had both started their naval careers at Dartmouth.

His training took him around the world to Gibraltar, Singapore, New Zealand, Tonga, Honolulu, San Francisco and Bermuda. He learned to be a helicopter pilot at the Royal Naval Air Station, Yeovilton, before joining 845 Naval Air Squadron as a pilot on board the commando carrier HMS *Hermes*.

In February 1976 Prince Charles was given his own ship, the minehunter HMS *Bronington*, which he commanded until the end of his active Royal Naval service in December 1976.

Prince Charles was just 20 years old when his mother, Her Majesty the Queen, invested him as Prince of Wales at Caernarfon Castle.

The Prince holds high ranks in the Royal Navy, the Army and the Royal Air Force. Here, dressed in naval uniform, with medals and garter star decoration, he takes the salute at a passing out parade at the Britannia Royal Naval College, Dartmouth.

The Prince of Wales is a title created for the male heir to the throne by Edward I in 1301 for his son, Edward II. There is no automatic succession to this title, but it is usually passed on when the existing Prince of Wales becomes King; then the title is renewed only if the Sovereign wishes. The Queen created her son, Prince Charles, Prince of Wales on 26 July 1958, though he was not invested until eleven years later.

Prince Charles' military uniform bears the famous wings badge of the Parachute Regiment, of which he is Colonel-in-Chief. When that appointment was made, in 1978, the Prince asked to take part in a parachute training course, so that he could wear the Regiment's famous beret and badge with justification.

~

His Royal Highness holds the ranks of Vice-Admiral in the Royal Navy, Air Marshal in the Royal Air Force and Lieutenant General in the Army. He holds honorary rank and appointments in many regiments.

Prince Charles wears military uniform as Lieutenant General of the Army as he attends St Paul's Cathedral for a memorial ceremony for service personnel who died in the Iraq conflict.

The famous blue wings of the Parachute Regiment can be seen on this military uniform worn by the Prince, who holds the Army rank of Lieutenant General, when he visited troops at Risborough Barracks, Kent.

Charles, a twenty-first-century prince

THERE IS NO FORMAL ROLE that accompanies the title Prince of Wales, yet Charles has proved to be a remarkably modern, active and innovative Prince, creating opportunities for work in many fields.

He is keenly interested in architecture, the environment, health and young people. Organic farming is now seen as a positive way forward for the agricultural industry – Prince Charles has supported natural methods of food production and conservation since the early part of 1980, long before they became mass consumer issues.

At Highgrove House, the Gloucestershire country residence that he bought in 1980, the year before his marriage to the late Diana, Princess of Wales, the Home Farm on the estate has been converted to organic methods in line with his fears about the use of artificial pesticides and chemicals.

He has put his ideas about energy conservation and traditional architecture into practice at Poundbury, the urban expansion on Duchy of Cornwall land to the west of Dorchester. Prince Charles has worked closely with the local authorities, architects and builders to ensure an exemplary addition to the ancient market town, where private and social housing are intermingled and built to the same high standard.

He has not only spoken of his concern that many young people are being denied access to fulfilling work, but has also done much to allay those concerns by establishing The Prince's Trust. This organization, founded in 1976, has allowed thousands of young people to set up their own businesses.

Prince Charles has long advocated a system of integrated healthcare where patients not only have access to conventional medical treatment but may also choose from complementary care such as homeopathy, acupuncture and herbal medicine. To this end he has established The Prince of Wales Foundation for Integrated Health with the aim of encouraging conventional and complementary medical practitioners to work together.

His working life has been spent in a personal exploration of what constitutes a civilized society and in setting up organizations to help people gain some of this advantage in their own lives. Prince Charles has always taken the long view and is seen by many as the voice of reason in an increasingly frenetic society. He has often said that he cares deeply about the future of all our children and grandchildren.

The bulk of his time is spent undertaking public engagements, in Britain and abroad. Recently his two sons, Princes William and Harry, who are second and third in line to the throne, have accompanied their father on some of his official visits.

Staff at the Crisis Skylight Café in London's East End enjoy a joke with the Prince, visiting in his role as President of Business in the Community.

Prince Charles is an active sportsman, inheriting the Royal Family's love of horses, riding and racing. He is a keen polo player and enjoys skiing, sailing and aqua-lung diving. He is patron of many arts organizations in which he takes a genuine interest, enjoying opera, music generally and the theatre. His talent for watercolour work has been of benefit to charity when his paintings have been sold in aid of organizations which he supports. Gardening is another love – he and the late plantswoman Rosemary Verey have created a garden of note at his country home, Highgrove House in Gloucestershire.

Prince Charles and Prince William inspect the Ayrshire herd on the Duchy Home Farm at Highgrove.

More than 360 organizations can call Prince Charles their patron or president. They include societies concerned with the interests of young people, the arts, conservation, sport, heritage, the unemployed, the disabled and the elderly, medicine, the environment and architecture.

~

The Prince works hard for his 17 core charities, most of which he founded and which are, in the main, concerned with young people, health, the environment, heritage, the arts, building design and business.

The Prince opens the Millennium Belvedere Tower, a central feature of the Poundbury development in Dorset.

Camilla – companion, wife and friend

THE EYES OF THE WORLD were on them, but the wedding of the Prince of Wales and Mrs Camilla Parker Bowles at Windsor was an occasion above all for family and close friends.

This is significant because the woman who became second in the country only to Her Majesty the Queen when she married the heir to the throne is a person known to value her privacy and shun public limelight.

Camilla Rosemary Shand, born in London on 17 July 1947 to wine merchant and Adjutant of the Yeomen of the Guard Major Bruce Shand and the Hon. Rosalind Cubitt, the daughter of Lord Ashcombe, was educated at Queen's Gate School in South Kensington, and in Switzerland and France. She took part in the London debutante season. Her close family upbringing, with a younger brother and sister at the Shand's estate in East Sussex, instilled the love of rural life, watercolour painting and country pursuits that she shares with Prince Charles.

She and the Prince have known each other since they met at a Windsor polo match in 1970, a year before Prince Charles joined the Royal Navy. They have remained friends since then.

Her marriage to Army officer Andrew Parker Bowles ended in 1995 and from that time she had lived at her Wiltshire home, enjoying the company of friends and family, including her two grown-up children, Tom and Laura. She is a strong person, self-confident, outgoing, charming, warm, funny and, in her relationship with Prince Charles, supportive and loyal – important qualities for the wife of the future King.

On marriage she became Her Royal Highness the Duchess of Cornwall, only the third woman in history to be known by that title. The first was Caroline of Ansbach, wife of George II, while the second was the wife of King George V, Mary of Teck. It is one of the titles that Camilla automatically received by marrying the Prince of Wales. She also became the Duchess of Rothesay, a title she uses in Scotland, a country she visits regularly and is known to love.

Camilla enjoys herself at a Society ball in March 1983.

Camilla received worldwide plaudits for her first public speech in Lisbon, Portugal, in May 2002 when she argued movingly the case for research and funding into osteoporosis, the crippling bone disease. She told an international conference on the disease that her mother, Rosalind Shand, and grandmother, Sonia Keppell, had both died of osteoporosis. She became patron of the National Osteoporosis Society in 1997, president in 2001 and has since done much to raise funds for education and research work.

Camilla chose two stunning outfits for her wedding to Prince Charles.

For the civil ceremony at Windsor Guildhall she wore an oyster silk basket-weave coat with herringbone stitch embroidery and a chiffon dress with appliqué detail, by Kensington fashion house Robinson Valentine.

Her natural straw hat, overlaid with ivory French lace and trimmed with feathers, was designed by Philip Treacy, as was the dramatic headdress of diamond-tipped gold-leafed feathers that she wore for the blessing at St George's Chapel. This second ceremony saw the Duchess wearing an elegant full length porcelain blue silk coat dress, also by Robinson Valentine, with hand-painted ikat design and gold thread embroidery.

The newly married couple leave Windsor Guildhall, their children happily congregating behind. The accessories chosen by the Duchess to enhance her outfit were a wide-brimmed hat, suede shoes and ivory clutch bag.

At the family home in East Sussex, Camilla was close to both her brother Mark and sister Annabel. Mark Shand is an explorer and award-winning travel writer whose books include the best-selling *River Dog* and *Travels on My Elephant*.

≈

When Prince Charles becomes King, his wife will become the first Princess Consort in British history. Her title echoes that of Queen Victoria's husband, Prince Albert, who was officially known as Prince Consort to The Queen.

Appropriately dressed for the occasion, Camilla arrives at the Royal Gala charity performance of Andrew Lloyd Webber's musical The Woman in White.

Charles and Camilla – sharing a life

A COUNTRY CHILDHOOD and a happy family upbringing taught Camilla Shand to enjoy outdoor pursuits and the value of a good sense of humour. She and Prince Charles share a love of all things rural. She is an excellent horsewoman while his prowess on horseback – especially on the polo field – is unquestioned. Camilla has always loved dogs and kept terriers at her Wiltshire home. Both she and the Prince know the therapeutic value of pulling on a pair of wellington boots and setting off for a relaxing walk in the countryside, an exercise especially precious for those subjected to constant public scrutiny.

The Duchess of Cornwall has a warm and witty personality with a sense of humour matching that of the Prince. Many photographs of the couple taken before and after their wedding show them enjoying a joke together, their laughter and their relaxed attitudes revealing their complete ease with each other. Both are comfortable in country tweeds and jodhpurs, while Prince Charles is quite at home wearing his Hunting Stewart or Balmoral Tartan kilt and carrying a shepherd's crook when attending events in Scotland. He and Camilla have attended the Mey Games in Caithness, northern Scotland, the Prince in his kilt, she wearing a matching green skirt and jacket, both hugely enjoying the traditional Highland dancing, piping and shot-putting.

Prince Charles is famously fond of gardens and gardening, another interest he shares with Camilla. She revealed her belief in the stress-relieving qualities of sowing, planting and pruning while chatting to a judge at the annual Sandringham Flower Show.

Just as calming is making time to sit quietly, absorbing a beautiful landscape and committing it to paper. The Prince is a watercolourist of talent and Camilla shares his ability. Both have painted for charity – a striking picture of a rhinoceros by the Duchess raised several hundred pounds for an animal charity.

The Prince of Wales has a taxing daily schedule of official visits, speeches to make and papers to study. The support of a wife who enjoys the same leisure pursuits, helps him to relax and shares his cares and concerns is invaluable, as is her presence at formal occasions.

The marriage of Prince Charles and Camilla Parker Bowles brought their four children, already good friends, closer together. Prince Charles is godfather to Tom Parker Bowles, who was born in 1974 and is now a successful food writer. Camilla's daughter, Laura, born in 1978, runs an art gallery in Belgravia. Eton- and Oxford-educated Tom and his sister, who went to Oxford Brooks University, made frequent visits to Highgrove, St James's Palace and Clarence House while they were growing up. Prince William, who is second in line to the throne, and his younger brother Prince Harry, also old Etonians, have spent much of their childhood moving in the same circles as the Parker Bowles children.

Prince Charles and Camilla in Marlborough, Wiltshire, where she showed the Prince new equipment bought for a crime prevention scheme of which she is a trustee.

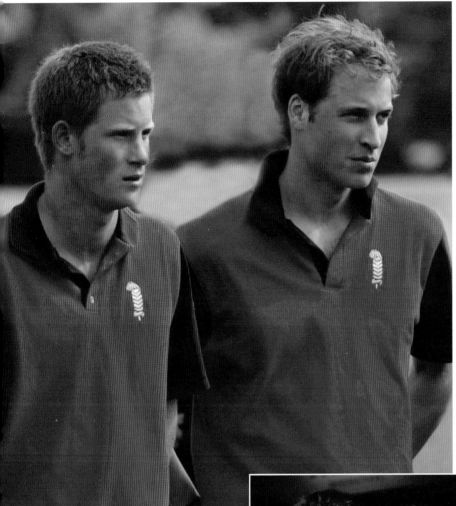

Regular visitors to watercolour exhibitions should keep their eyes open for works by Arthur George Carrick. This is a pseudonym sometimes used by Prince Charles, using two of his Christian names and part of his title Earl of Carrick.

Horse riding is a favourite form of relaxation for Camilla.

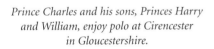

Prince Charles and his sons, Princes Harry and William, enjoy polo at Cirencester in Gloucestershire.

Prince William and Prince Harry were told of their father's engagement to Camilla several weeks before the news was made public. They both expressed their pleasure, later issuing a joint statement: *We are both very happy for our father and Camilla and we wish them all the luck in the future.*

Camilla and her children, Tom and Laura Parker Bowles, arrive at a book launch for Tom.

A honeymoon in Scotland

BEFORE PLUNGING BACK into his busy official schedule, Prince Charles and his new wife honeymooned at their secluded country retreat on the Royal Balmoral estate in Scotland. Birkhall, a whitewashed Jacobean hunting lodge, bequeathed to the Prince by his late grandmother, has been described as his favourite home. He spent many of his childhood holidays in this wonderful Highland setting, learning to fish in the River Muick that runs through the bottom of the two-acre garden and enjoying the splendid views. More recently he and the Duchess redecorated the 12-bedroom property in comfortable chintzy country-house style to reflect their love of rural life.

Birkhall was a favourite home of the Queen Mother who added a new wing in the 1950s and who designed the magnificent flower garden with her husband King George VI. Now her grandson is completing her work and is introducing organic methods of cultivation to this beautiful Deeside garden. As a memorial to her, an 18th-century style gazebo has been built in the grounds. A chalet in the nearby pine woods gives fine views of the Prince's favourite Scottish peak, Lochnagar.

The couple are very likely to pay many visits to the Castle of Mey during their marriage. This castle with its magnificent gardens was bought and restored by the Queen Mother soon after the death of her husband King George VI in 1952. She saw the isolated and dilapidated Barrogill Castle, overlooking the Pentland Firth, gave it back its original name and set about the renovation. The Castle now belongs to a Trust and is open to the public, but the Prince visits at least once a year, renting it during August.

Birkhall, the honeymoon destination for the Royal couple, is said to be Prince Charles' favourite home.

Prince Charles and his wife enjoy visiting the Castle of Mey overlooking the Pentland Firth in Scotland. The magnificent gardens were restored by the late Queen Mother.

The countryside around Balmoral generally, and the fine peak of Lochnagar in particular, made a great impression on Prince Charles during his formative years. When he was a young man he wrote a children's book, *The Old Man of Lochnagar*, to amuse his young brothers, Princes Andrew and Edward, during a family trip on the Royal Yacht *Britannia*. The book – which begins with the words: *Not all that long ago when children were even smaller and people had especially hairy knees, there lived an old man of Lochnagar* – was later published with illustrations by Sir Hugh Casson, and turned into a stage play.

The Duchy for which the Duchess of Cornwall is named is a 600-year-old estate, created by Edward III for his son the Black Prince, and covering more than 141,000 acres, half of them on Dartmoor in Devon. The Duchy, which also owns most of the land on the Isles of Scilly, provides an income for the public and private life of Prince Charles, who receives no allowance from the Civil List. He has encouraged his tenant farmers to protect and conserve the environment, holding regular Habitat Awards to reward good practice. Organic products, including sausages, bacon, biscuits, chutneys, chocolates and drinks, made to the highest conservation standards on Duchy farms, are sold to raise money for the Prince's charities.

At their first official duty as a married couple, the Duke and Duchess of Rothesay
open a play park at Ballater during their honeymoon.

Town and country – the official homes

CLARENCE HOUSE, the imposing mansion built in 1825 by John Nash for the Duke of Clarence, became the official London residence of Prince Charles after the death of the Queen Mother.

He and Princes William and Harry moved into the classically proportioned stuccoed building next door to York House, their previous London home inside St James's Palace, on 4 August 2003. Although Clarence House had undergone extensive refurbishment before the Princes moved in, the atmosphere of a much-loved family house has been retained. Prince Charles, his wife and the young princes enjoy new colour schemes, fresh textiles and newly chosen works of art from the Royal Collection. The Prince has enriched the decoration with favourite pieces from his own collection. But perhaps the most interesting paintings are those once owned by the Queen Mother, including works by John Piper, Walter Sickert, Graham Sutherland and Augustus John.

The Prince and the Duchess share part of their home with the public for a few weeks each year, when the main rooms on the ground floor open between August and the middle of October.

Hosting important gatherings comes easily to the Prince's wife who helps her husband receive important guests and official visitors in the principal rooms of the house. Clarence House also provides offices for the official staff of the Prince of Wales who support him in his official engagements and liaise with the hundreds of organizations with which he is involved.

When the Royal couple are not in London, there's every chance they are at their country home, Highgrove House, near Tetbury in Gloucestershire. Bought by the Duchy of Cornwall on behalf of the Prince of Wales in 1980, Highgrove once belonged to MP Maurice Macmillan, son of the former Prime Minister.

It is perfectly situated for the Prince; London is only an hour or so away while the southern and western counties, where the Duchy has most of its properties, are on the doorstep.

In keeping with Prince Charles' architectural preferences, Highgrove is built of stone with a neo-classical façade. It is the smallest of his residences with six principal bedrooms and four reception rooms. The Orchard Room, a new Cotswold-stone building in the grounds, is where he hosts many of his meetings.

The Duchess of Cornwall shares the Prince's enjoyment of gardening and it is here, at Highgrove, that she is able to indulge this pleasure. Prince Charles has had the help of several plantswomen in creating this now famous garden; the Dowager Marchioness of Salisbury helped him with the initial structure and the rose garden, while wildflower expert, the late Miriam Rothschild, was instrumental on the sowing of the carpet of colour that greets visitors as they drive up to the house. His most famous collaboration was with the late Rosemary Verey whose advice helped the Prince to turn the whole garden into a plantsman's paradise.

> Home Farm at Highgrove is where the Prince of Wales has put his organic principles into practice. By 1996 the whole farm, the home of the Prince's organic food business, Duchy Originals, had received full organic status.

Summer visitors to Highgrove House are greeted by this magnificent display of wild flowers.

Clarence House, once the home of the late Queen Elizabeth the Queen Mother, is now the official London residence of Prince Charles and his family.

During HM the Queen Mother's residence at Clarence House it became the custom for the Royal Family to gather there on 4 August each year for a traditional birthday appearance. Hundreds of well-wishers crowded into Stable Yard Road outside the Royal residence to see the Queen Mother and to offer her birthday greetings, presents and flowers. Following her death in 2002, Clarence House underwent extensive redecoration before Prince Charles and his family moved in, on the anniversary of her birthday.

A corner of the Garden Room at Clarence House, with a painting of Noah's Ark by Leandro Bassano and a bust of Queen Elizabeth the Queen Mother, when she was Duchess of York, by Arthur Walker.

Their future together

HIS ROYAL HIGHNESS the Prince of Wales and his wife walked side by side down the aisle of St George's Chapel, Windsor Castle, on their wedding day to receive a blessing for their life together from the Archbishop of Canterbury, Dr Rowan Williams.

Earlier that day they exchanged wedding rings and had been joined as husband and wife at a civil ceremony held at Windsor's historic Guildhall.

Those watching the ceremony and The Queen's guests joined them at the reception afterwards in nearby Windsor Castle to wish them every happiness.

Prince Charles, the heir to the throne, has been brought up with a keen sense of duty. His role as King-in-waiting has not always been an easy one, yet he has created a life that gives much more than it takes. His has been the voice of reason, warning of the need for balance, the danger of throwing out all that is tried and tested for the sake of profit. He has established charities which support young people and the disadvantaged.

The Duchess of Cornwall has proved herself sensible and discreet. She is self-confident, warm, amusing, capable and, above all, supportive of the man she loves.

She shares Prince Charles' enjoyment of rural life but she is just as much at home hosting a reception, attending official engagements or making a speech at a charity occasion.

When Prince Charles becomes King, Camilla, his wife and Consort, will be by his side offering love and support in equal measure.

The British people may have every confidence that this couple will carry out their Royal duties meticulously, upholding the traditional values they both represent.

Prince Charles and Camilla both have a lively sense of humour.
Here they enjoy a joke at the Mey Highland Games.